O9-ABI-897

Plains Outbreak Tornadoes

Titles in the *American Disasters* series:

The Exxon Valdez
Tragic Oil Spill
ISBN 0-7660-1058-9

Hurricane Andrew
Nature's Rage
ISBN 0-7660-1057-0

The Oklahoma City Bombing
Terror in the Heartland
ISBN 0-7660-1061-9

Plains Outbreak Tornadoes
Killer Twisters
ISBN 0-7660-1059-7

San Francisco Earthquake, 1989
Death and Destruction
ISBN 0-7660-1060-0

The World Trade Center Bombing
Terror in the Towers
ISBN 0-7660-1056-2

Plains Outbreak Tornadoes

Killer Twisters

Victoria Sherrow

Enslow Publishers, Inc.

44 Fadem Road   PO Box 38
Box 699   Aldershot
Springfield, NJ 07081 Hants GU12 6BP
USA   UK

Copyright © 1998 by Enslow Publishers, Inc.

Library of Congress Cataloging-in-Publication Data

Sherrow, Victoria.
    Plains outbreak tornadoes: killer twisters / Victoria Sherrow.
        p. cm. — (American disasters)
    Includes bibliographical references and index.
    Summary: Details the series of destructive tornadoes that struck
the American Midwest during the span of several hours in April 1991,
causing severe damage in several states.
    ISBN 0-7660-1059-7
    1. Tornadoes—Middle West—Juvenile literature. [1. Tornadoes—
Middle West.] I. Title II. Series
QC955.5.U6S54   1998
363.34'923'0978—dc21   97-39180
                                            CIP
                                            AC

Printed in the United States of America

10 9 8 7 6 5 4 3 2 1

Photo Credits: AP/Wide World Photos, pp. 1, 6, 8, 10, 12, 17, 20, 22, 24, 26, 27, 29, 31, 34, 35, 37, 38, 39, 41.

Cover Photo: AP/Wide World Photos

Contents

CHAPTER 1

Night of Terror

Newsman Gregg Jarrett had lived in Kansas for more than two years without seeing a tornado. On April 26, 1991, he witnessed a raging funnel cloud firsthand. Jarrett was on the road with a fellow reporter for KSNW-Wichita. The two men were following another story when they spotted the tornado. They grabbed the camera, and Jarrett began describing the storm on tape. This would be a great piece of footage to take back to the newsroom.

Suddenly, the twister was heading right toward them. Jarrett later said, "We jumped into the car and I drove and my photographer Ted Lewis was hanging out the window with the camera rolling. . . ."[1] The men speeded up, trying to outrun the dark, twisting cloud. They hoped to reach an overpass they saw up ahead.

The newsmen urged people to leave their cars. They all took cover under the overpass. "Hang on to the girders!" Jarrett told the terrified group that had gathered around him.[2]

Jarrett and Lewis knew they were in grave danger.

They might not survive the storm. Jarrett said they told each other, "We are going to get this story even if we don't make it."[3]

The group watched as the twister spun closer and closer. Soon it reached the overpass. People clung to the girders and pressed their bodies to the concrete. Children screamed as the funnel cloud whizzed by.

> It sounded like a freight train. It just passed right on top of us. People are very upset. They're still hanging on, hanging

Two men sift through the rubble of what use to be a house in Andover, Kansas. A devastating tornado there left several people dead and more than two hundred injured.

on for their lives. It was a tremendous rush! Flying debris everywhere. Some people look to me like they're all right but they have scratches and bruises.[4]

The group under the overpass watched in horror as the twister hit a car that was still on the road. Swirling winds scooped up the car and threw it about two hundred yards. Jarrett called it "a mangled wreckage."[5] He rushed to aid two people. They had been thrown from the car. Jarrett later said, "There were trucks and tractor-trailer rigs strewn all over the highway for about 50, 60 miles. The devastation was unbelievable."[6]

Other places were also devastated. Within a few hours, more than ten twisters touched down in south central Kansas alone. More than fifty tornadoes hit Kansas and five other states (Iowa, Nebraska, Missouri, Kansas, Oklahoma, and Texas). Fierce winds bent huge trees in their path. The violent funnel clouds knocked down homes. They ripped apart roofs and walls, then sucked up the contents—chairs, tables, beds, appliances. The storms left more than twenty people dead and hundreds of others injured.

Severe storms are not new to people who live in the tornado belt that cuts across the Midwest. Tornado Alley is the region with the most frequent tornado activity. The "Alley" begins in Texas and moves north into Oklahoma, Kansas, and Iowa. People living in this region hear dozens of tornado watches and warnings each year. Funnel clouds are frequently seen on the American plains from the spring through the fall. But this 1991 outbreak was even worse than usual.

Some people in the hardest-hit areas said they had never seen such severe tornadoes. A man in Andover, Kansas, compared the destruction with a city that had been bombed hundreds of times. He said, "Looks like London did over there in World War II."[7] One reporter called it "unlike anything anyone could remember."[8]

A funnel cloud spins across the ground near Jarrell, Texas. Texas was one of the states to be hit by the outbreak of tornadoes in 1991.

CHAPTER 2

Whirling Windstorms

In the 1939 movie *The Wizard of Oz*, a twister picks up a Kansas farmhouse. It carries the house, Dorothy, and her dog, Toto, far away to a land of witches, Munchkins, and talking animals. The movie is fiction, but tornadoes can do amazing things. One Oklahoma couple was taken for a "ride" inside their home. The tornado destroyed the walls and roof, but the floor stayed together. The couple was unhurt when their house was returned to the ground.

In 1947, a car with two passengers was carried in the air for about two hundred feet. Then, it was set back down. Amazingly, the men were not injured.

In another case, a funnel cloud sucked up a railroad car. The car was turned around in midair. It landed on the ground on a different track, facing the other way. During an earlier tornado, a train was also blown off the tracks. Railroad workers never saw the train again. It may have been smashed into pieces that were then scattered across the prairie.

*T*ornadoes are capable of blowing cars off the road. This overturned car in Andover, Kansas, serves as a reminder of the damage a tornado can cause.

Another bizarre event occurred in 1986 when a tornado hit Sweetwater, Texas. A police officer stopped to help a victim whose car had been blown off the road. The car's rear windows were gone. Officer Carnathan recalled, "There was a kitten lying in the back seat, all wet. So I told the woman we would take care of her cat for her. And she said, 'I don't have a cat!' Then this fellow comes walking down the street holding two other kittens and looking for the third one."[1]

The word tornado comes from a Spanish word, *tronada*, which means thunderstorm. Tornadoes are circular windstorms that originate from thunderstorms. The conditions that lead to these storms are especially violent. What are those conditions? Tornadoes develop near low-pressure areas of high winds. The atmosphere close to the earth's surface is constantly moving. Different regions are warmer or cooler than other places. This depends on their position in relation to the sun, cloud cover, and other things. As air becomes warmer, it expands and becomes lighter in weight. Warmer air moves upward.

When two very different masses of air bump into each other, the thunderstorms that generate tornadoes are formed. Fast-moving, cold dry air meets moister, warmer air. Usually, cold air moves underneath warmer air. In this case, though, the cold air mass overruns the warmer air. The warm air then rushes upward at fast speeds. Air also blows in from the sides. This creates strong, twisting updrafts. The core of low pressure becomes a tornado. This low-pressure area acts like a powerful vacuum.

Like hurricanes, tornadoes have two kinds of motion. Their winds rotate, twirling around a center. Tornadoes usually spin counterclockwise in the Northern Hemisphere and clockwise in the Southern Hemisphere. As they spin, tornadoes also move forward. Wind speeds at the end of the funnel cloud sometimes may reach 280 miles per hour.

The combination of rapid winds and a low-pressure core can cause tremendous damage. One midwesterner who has seen a dozen tornadoes compares them to "a huge vacuum cleaner."[2]

Funnel clouds vary in color and their center is made up of tiny droplets of water. After touching down, the funnel typically becomes darker as dirt and various objects are sucked into the twisting winds. The tornado may pick up dust, rocks, tree limbs, and parts of buildings.

This debris also acts on things the funnel cloud hits. The winds can ram objects like doors, or even pieces of straw, into thick tree trunks. The powerful winds can even tear the feathers from chickens.

A reporter described the scene after a tornado ripped through the town of Barneveld, Wisconsin, in 1984.

> Smashed glass glistened in the streets. Bedsheets dangled from trees. A fork protruded from the brick wall of the firehouse. Dead songbirds lay on the ground, completely stripped of their feathers. Old Christmas decorations sparkled in the road.[3]

People who had been tossed hundreds of feet by the

winds suffered from cracked skulls, broken limbs, and knocked-out teeth.

Tornadoes range in width from a few meters to as much as two kilometers wide at the ground. The average tornado is about one hundred meters wide. Some tornadoes travel only a few dozen meters; others rise and fall over dozens of kilometers.

At the end of its life cycle, which may last from a few seconds to several hours, the funnel cloud is drawn back up into the parent thunderstorm. A thunderstorm may produce a second tornado minutes or even hours after the first one. Tornadoes may also contain more than one circulation spinning around their middle. These are called multiple vortex tornadoes.

Tornadoes are hard to predict and there is rarely a typical tornado. For example, the average tornado travels at about twenty to thirty miles per hour. Yet some travel at sixty miles per hour or more. Most tornadoes move from southwest to northeast, or from west to east. They have been known to move in any direction, however. Some have even made a complete circle. Other tornadoes make sudden turns.

Before the twister itself appears, green lightning can be seen in the sky. Rumbling sounds are heard. Clouds come nearer, and the thunder turns into a roar. Lightning flashes as the cloud spins in the air.

Wherever a high-speed twister hits, it is likely to cause severe damage. The average length of a tornado's path is slightly more than four miles. When the tornado is over, large marks can be seen on the ground. The marks may be semicircular, like scoops laid next to one another.

Tornadoes usually occur in the afternoon, when thunderstorms grow in the hottest period of the day. However, these storms can occur any time of the day or night. Tornadoes occur throughout the world. But the United States has more tornadoes, and more of the most violent tornadoes, than any other country. More than one thousand tornadoes form in the United States each year. During some years there are far more than the average number.

Although tornadoes often form in the Midwest, they can happen in any state. Massachusetts has the highest average number of tornado deaths per ten thousand square miles. Delaware has the highest concentration of tornadoes that result in injuries. According to the Federal Emergency Management Agency (FEMA), "Tornadoes are nature's most violent storms. . . . Every state is at some risk from this hazard."[4]

Most tornadoes occur on land. However, similar twisting windstorms can also take place at sea. These are called waterspouts. Hailstones often occur with tornadoes. These chunks of ice can become as large as tennis balls or even grapefruits. They start when bits of ice and dust combine with cold water in the air. These balls of ice, dust, and water freeze. They increase in size as they hit more water droplets. These small ice chunks are tossed around in the storm, and grow larger over time. Finally, they fall to the earth.

Hailstones add to the damage caused by tornadoes. They strike grasses, plants, crops, cars, and buildings. These balls of ice can break windows and destroy roofs. Large hailstones can injure or kill animals and even people.

*T*ornadoes usually occur in the afternoon, when thunderstorms (like the one seen here) grow in the hottest period of the day.

As a tornado finishes its run, its circulation begins to fall apart. The funnel becomes narrow and twisted, like a rope, trailing the thunderhead from which it came. The twister becomes thinner and thinner until it disappears. It leaves behind a trail of destruction.

Scientists do not know how to stop tornadoes before they begin on their harmful course. The best they can do is spot these killer storms in time to warn people in threatened areas. On the afternoon of April 26, 1991, numerous tornado warnings had been issued in Kansas as funnel clouds darted across the state.

Running for Cover

Sirens clanged as tornado warning systems went off at McConnell Air Force Base near Wichita, Kansas. The base was founded in 1951 and developed into a Tactical Air Command Base. It was a large and important military installation. During the 1960s, Titan II intercontinental ballistic missiles were housed there. During the 1980s, the base was home to the B-1B Lancer bomber.

Hearing the sirens, people hurried to shelters built to protect people during tornadoes. The tornado ripped across the base, traveling southwest to northeast. It knocked down dozens of power lines. Property damage was extensive. The twister destroyed 102 housing units and nine other facilities. They included the hospital and most of McConnell's service buildings. Ten facilities suffered minor damage.[1]

Luckily, the tornado sidestepped a line of B-1 bombers. These planes were worth a total of about one billion dollars. It also missed a large parking lot full of cars. Nobody was killed, and only sixteen people were injured. People had responded promptly to the warning.

The storm had arrived at McConnell as what is called a single vortex tornado. By the time it left, the tornado had become more deadly. It had become a multiple vortex tornado, with more than one circulation inside the original tornado. This tornado was part of a series of twisters that hit several communities in Kansas. They included Andover, Clearwater, El Dorado, Haysville, and Wichita.

*A*irmen work to remove a car from the hospital doorway at McConnell Air Force Base in Wichita, Kansas.

In Andover, the tornado warning system did not work properly. Some tornado sirens failed to go off. The mayor of Andover found out about the problem and sent out police and fire units. They visited neighborhoods and warned residents that a tornado had been spotted. They urged people to take cover.

More than two hundred people in the Golden Spur Trailer Park in Andover responded to the warnings. They took cover in a tornado shelter. Others did not heed the warning, however. One policeman who sounded an alarm in a trailer park videotaped as he went along. The tape showed that some people continued strolling through the neighborhood. Others were walking their dogs. They did not seem too concerned about the storm.

Meanwhile, the tornado continued on its deadly path. It was moving over the land like a freight train. A terrifying roar filled the air. People compared the sound with hundreds of jet planes or locomotives. Lightning flashed. Rains and hailstones pounded the ground. The tornado looked like a large, billowing funnel of smoke.

Guber Lecky and his son and daughter-in-law were in the basement of their home in Andover when the twister hit. They crouched together as the savage winds raged above them. Within seconds, it ripped the house right off its foundation.

The family was grateful to be alive after the storm had gone. They later found out that fourteen people in their community had died. The outbreak of tornadoes that night would cause the deaths of twenty-one people in Kansas and Oklahoma.

The Golden Spur mobile home park was left in ruins. People feared there were victims buried in the piles of rubble. Carol Smith lived in this park. She recalled, "The lady next door to me, you could hear her screaming underneath the debris, right there."[2]

Inside the Golden Spur park, 1,230 trailers had been mowed down. Elsewhere in town, 110 homes were

A motor home lies on its roof, after a devestating tornado passed through.

destroyed.[3] More than one thousand people in Andover alone were now homeless.[4]

The tornado continued to wreck havoc along its path. Several people were killed and injured on the highways. One man was driving his truck when the twister hit. The truck rolled over five to six times before stopping alongside the road. The driver was visibly shaken as he spoke with newsman Greg Jarrett. He said, "You can't describe it." The man looked up toward the sky, saying, "I'd like to be alone for a few minutes. I've got some thanking to do."[5]

Nearby, emergency vehicles arrived at this scene to treat the injured. Quick medical attention saved the life of an unconscious man who lay on the highway. He was rushed to the hospital.

Emergency crews also sped to the Golden Spur trailer park and other hard-hit areas. Red Cross workers arrived in Andover and Wichita to begin relief work.

As dawn broke on April 27, people in the stricken region faced many problems. Some grieved for dead friends or family members. Others waited anxiously for news of loved ones who were injured. Homeless people looked for temporary housing. Some of these hundreds of men, women, and children went to stay with family or friends. Others sought help from local churches and public shelters.

Some fortunate people in the region had escaped the tornado's fury. They reached out to help others. People arrived at churches and shelters with donations of food and clothing.

A few people worriedly sought missing relatives. Robert Minenger's family could not find him. Minenger had lived at the Golden Spur trailer park. His wife and daughter had been away from the trailer park when the tornado hit. They feared he had died and was buried in the rubble. The family waited and hoped as search teams combed the debris at the park.

A woman from Andover, Kansas, displays a family album found in the debris of her mobile home.

CHAPTER 4

"Everybody Cares"

Members of the National Guard joined police search teams looking for victims. These teams worked for days, searching. An Andover city official said that the search was difficult. The teams had to work quickly and were dealing with large quantities of debris. The official said, "You're looking for needles in haystacks. . . ."[1]

Robert Minenger was still missing two days after the tornado had hit. His family wanted to go inside the trailer park to search for him. Officials told people to stay away while professional search teams were still working. This was frustrating for the family. Mike Warren was Minenger's son-in-law. Warren told a TV newsman, "They never would let us in here. I just wanted to come over here you know."[2]

On Sunday, people were allowed to go into the park. Former residents of the park searched for belongings that had not been destroyed. Robert Minenger's family was devastated when they discovered his body in the rubble.

National Guardsmen march into a mobile home park to search for bodies.

Rescue workers had been digging in that same area just before 4:00 P.M. that day. At that time, the workers were ordered to stop for the day.

Pat Murphy and her family were out of town on the night of the tornado. They returned to Andover on Sunday, April 28. Their home had been turned into piles of debris on a broken foundation. Murphy had decided to bring her children, Angela and Taylor, to the scene. She had told the children about the tornado. But they did not really understand what had happened. Murphy said, "They just don't realize all their toys are just gone."[3]

Restaurant owner Bob Livingston had survived that frightening night in Andover. The tornado destroyed the building that housed his restaurant. Livingston managed

*T*his overturned red wagon serves as a reminder of all the things that are destroyed or lost in the devastation of a tornado.

to save some of his supplies and equipment, however. He expressed great surprise at the random damage the storm had caused. After the tornado, he found unbroken eggs in what had once been his restaurant. Livingston showed the eggs to reporters. He said, "Look at the trailer over there. That's the frame off of a trailer, and it's just mangled. And yet an egg survives and doesn't even crack."[4]

On Saturday, the two United States senators and some of the representatives from Kansas toured the stricken area. Senators Bob Dole and Nancy Kassebaum met with Governor Joan Finney. They promised that the federal government would send help.

The victims appreciated government aid and other help. They faced a huge, exhausting task, however. As Guber Lecky said, "Cleaning up your hopes and dreams, that's difficult."[5]

Damage to the state exceeded $20 million. Governor Finney declared Andover a disaster area. President George Bush agreed to send millions of dollars in federal funds to aid victims. State officials canceled activities that had been planned for that week. One of them was a parade on Sunday to welcome veterans back home from the Persian Gulf War, which had just ended.

That day, people gathered at churches for memorial services. They prayed for tornado victims and their families. In Andover, congregations grieved for the fourteen people who had died. Members of the Catholic church no longer had a building to hold services, however. It had been crushed by the tornado.

Teachers at local schools worried about students who were still not accounted for and may have died or been injured. Carol Musick taught second graders at Andover Elementary School. She told reporters, "What's really hard in all this, every kid, every one of them, is our kid. We still don't know how many of them are gone." The principal, Bob Martin, said, "I've been here 18 years, and I know a

*W*reckage and the outer walls of a church (near Andover) are all that remain following a devastating tornado.

lot of the people and a lot of the kids in that trailer court."[6]

In the weeks after the tornado, mental health professionals visited schools. Psychologists and counselors tried to help teachers and students adjust to the disaster.

People had a lot of extra work to do during those weeks. Dump trucks and bulldozers had begun cleaning up some areas soon after the storms ended. Residents were given a few days to search for their belongings before bulldozers were sent to clean up. Among those who came searching was the Bartlett family. They had lived in the Golden Spur trailer park for nearly a year. After the tornado, they looked for any usable household items or keepsakes in the rubble. Lonie Bartlett showed CBS correspondent James Hattori some photographs she had found. They were pictures taken after her wedding ceremony in May 1990. Bartlett told Hattori, "We just started getting settled good, things starting to look good."[7]

Beverly Finney and her husband lost everything they owned. Finney returned to the trailer park on Saturday afternoon, April 27, to see what she could recover. She said, "I was able to salvage our wedding pictures and a couple of unbroken glass pieces."[8] The Finneys found another trailer to move into in nearby Benton, Kansas.

People had only a few days to recover what they could before bulldozers were sent in. Some returned daily until the rubble was completely cleared away. They searched for anything that was worth saving.

Rose and Paul Skafe had lost their home in Andover.

Each day, they came back to their shattered neighborhood. Their neighbors were searching the ruins for household goods and mementos. The elderly Skafes were too weak and sickly to search on their own. Neighbors helped them to recover some belongings. Linda Wallace was among these good-hearted people. She told a reporter that she felt a need to help other victims. Wallace said, "This is my community."[9]

People from around the country also felt a desire to

A man walks out of his basement, as the rest of his home barely remains standing in Andover, Kansas.

help the tornado victims. They sent money and clothing to the stricken area. Piles of clothing were placed in the Andover Elementary School gym and in Sunday school classrooms at the United Methodist Church. People came to these centers to find replacements for clothing they had lost.

Tons of food were also sent to Andover. Local churches asked their members to donate food. The gym at the Andover Elementary School was turned into a warehouse to hold all the food. Volunteers arrived to sort and distribute it. Some of these volunteers were people who stayed to help after they had brought donations. Patty Bagsail was among them. She said, "Everybody cares. I wouldn't live anyplace else."[10]

CHAPTER 5

Restoring Communities

A spirit of kindness and cooperation helped many communities to mend after the devastating Kansas tornadoes of April 26, 1991. People in hard-hit areas like Andover, Kansas, faced months of rebuilding. Electricity and other utilities were restored to the area within two weeks. Housing remained a problem for months, though. People had to adjust to many changes in their lives.

People in north central Oklahoma were somewhat more fortunate. The tornado that hit Billings and Red Rock on April 26 had been vicious. Its total path length was some sixty-six miles. Yet this was a sparsely populated area. Only six people were injured and nobody was killed. The storm did about $500,000 worth of damage.[1]

The help and compassion shown by others boosted victims' spirits. School principal Bob Martin said, "If there is any good to come out of this, it's the fact that the people of Kansas always rally in something like this. They're super."[2]

People who had lost their homes filed insurance claims. Some of them used their insurance payments to rebuild in the same town or area. Others decided they would move away. Paul and Juanita Perryman had seen their trailer home of eleven years destroyed by the storm. Mrs. Perryman told a newsman that the couple would probably buy a home in Wichita now. They did not want to face this kind of risk again.

Restaurant owner Bob Livingston worked hard to restore his business in a different building. He said, "I was never really afraid of tornadoes till now. Now I am. I mean, it puts the fear in you."[3]

At McConnell Air Force Base, the rebuilding process went on for years. Congress agreed the base could have $55 million for repairs and new building. A great deal of work was done during the last months of 1991. New building projects had been planned even before the storm

*T*his photo shows the extent of damage that can result following the fierce wind and rain of a tornado.

hit. Now, the base had to replace its hospital as quickly as possible. Workers also began building new housing units to replace those that were destroyed.[4]

During the next two years, a new lodging facility and skills development center went up. By 1994, 102 housing units were completed at McConnell. A new $17 million Medical Treatment Facility was opened in March 1994. That August people at the base were glad to have a new center, which became known as Emerald City. This large new facility included lounges and dining rooms, a swimming pool, a fitness center, and a bowling alley. Several of the old recreational centers had been destroyed during the storm.[5]

It was hard to believe that something that passed

*I*t is hard to believe that something that passes through an area as quickly as most tornadoes do can cause so much destruction.

through the area so fast could cause so much damage. But tornadoes do. These storms rarely last more than twenty minutes. However, they kill dozens of people each year in the United States alone.

Scientists continue to study these whirling windstorms on tape. Numerous tapes have been made of twisters. The first known film footage was made in 1953. People called "storm chasers" also get close to tornadoes in order to film them. In May 1985 Ron Alfredo made the first known home video of a tornado. He was visiting relatives who lived near Hermitage, Pennsylvania. That tornado outbreak killed seven people. It was the worst ever to hit the state.

In June 1992 in Fritsch, Texas, a homeowner tried to film a tornado. The film shows trailers being knocked apart. As the man's house was hit, a piece of debris hit his head. He was knocked unconscious.

A number of people used camcorders to film the tornadoes that streaked across Kansas and Oklahoma on April 26, 1991. These videotapes let people see the enormous funnel clouds and get a feel for the intense roar of the tornado. One returning Gulf War veteran, a pilot, was among those who filmed the tornado in Kansas. Many people feared he would be hurt by going too near to the funnel cloud.

Professor Jerry Straka is an experienced storm chaser. He says, "There are a lot of people who talk big about tornado chasing and then, when they see a tornado, they chicken out. Look, I don't think people realize, really, how big they are. Even a small tornado is very big. . . . When you start seeing big chunks of debris flying around, you have second thoughts."[6]

Storm chasers still take these risks to study tornadoes, however. Professor Bluestein and his team filmed the tornado of April 26, 1991, near Red Rock, Oklahoma. At that time, Doppler radar measured the wind speed of the tornado at 287 miles per hour. This was the highest wind speed ever recorded for a tornado.[7]

*C*leanup efforts are under way after a tornado destroyed this home in Jarrell, Texas.

Some experts fear that a tornado may one day strike a large city or hit a place where many people have gathered. Allen Pearson is a former director of the National Severe Storms Forecast Center (NSSFC) in Norman, Oklahoma. He worries about the chance that a tornado might strike a sports stadium, rock concert, fairground, or the Indianapolis 500.[8] Author Keay Davidson wonders, "What would happen if a tornado struck a chemical plant, pesticide factory, or other toxic facility? . . . Might authorities be forced to evacuate communities, perhaps even entire regions, to protect people from the deadly whirlwind of poisons?"[9]

People do not know how to stop tornadoes. Perhaps

A car covered in rubble stands as a reminder of the damage caused by tornadoes.

they never will. At one time, scientists hoped to find a way to change or control the course of a storm. They wondered if they might find ways to spread out a tornado's power over a longer period. Now this is thought to be impossible.

Instead, scientists continue to look for better ways to understand and predict the weather. Early tornado warnings save lives, as hurricane warnings do. For example,

*T*he building on the left was four stories tall before a fierce tornado struck it.

nobody died when a savage tornado ripped across Oklahoma City on April 30, 1970. Civil Defense Director Hansen said, "It's just a miracle."[10]

Early warnings also saved lives in Oklahoma in 1986. A tornado hit the area around Oklahoma City and Edmond on May 8. It destroyed 30 homes and damaged 193 others. Yet nobody was killed or seriously hurt. Weather satellites at the National Weather Service showed a line of storms stretching from Texas to Kansas. A tornado watch was issued in the afternoon. A warning went out that evening before the tornado hit at 7:18 P.M. People took cover in their bathtubs and under their beds. One survivor said of the tornado, "I heard it roar through the chimney and felt it sucking things up. When we stood up, there was no roof."[11]

The National Weather Service can now give people warnings earlier than ever before. It uses satellites, radar, and computers to track storms and predict their course.

After the Plains outbreak of 1991, people were deeply concerned about the deaths that occurred in Andover. Officials would later investigate why the alarm system did not work properly. People complained that more lives could have been saved if the system had operated better.

Officials also stressed the need to respond quickly when a tornado alarm is issued. A number of local employees take action when disastrous weather threatens. Police, firefighters, rangers, and street crews are called on to spread the word.

People who live in tornado-prone areas have learned

ways to protect themselves. They may use public shelters. For now, the best way to handle an oncoming tornado is to run for cover. James McDonald, a civil engineer at the Institute for Disaster Reasearch, agrees. He said, "You want to put as many walls as possible between you and

*T*ornadoes can destroy communities and are especially devastating to the people who are forced to cope with their effects.

the outside."[12] People are urged to go below ground level in a cellar or basement and stay beneath a heavy table or stairwell. Some homes have no cellar or other area beneath the ground. If that is the case, people should go to the center of the house and stay in a closet or small room. Covering oneself with a blanket or heavy towels gives some protection against flying glass. James McDonald pointed out, "The greatest threat to individuals comes from flying objects such as broken glass, pipes, and lumber."[13]

Surviving a tornado is an unforgettable experience. Victims are haunted by the sights and sounds of these killer storms. Like other tornado victims, many people in Andover had nightmares after April 26, 1991. Children were especially affected. Parents said their children became terrified during stormy weather. Some victims said that in the months after the tornado they felt tired and experienced more illnesses. Others said they had been fine right after the storm, but began to feel fearful weeks or months later. People also worried about being separated from their loved ones during bad weather. They described feeling helpless in the face of such an awesome force of nature.

One survivor in Kansas said, "You see it on TV, but you don't — you don't really think it can happen until . . . it does."[14]

Other Major Tornadoes in United States History

DATE	PLACE	DEATHS
May 7, 1840	near Natchez, Mississippi	317
June 3, 1860	Iowa and Illinois	111
April 18, 1880	Marshfield, Missouri	99
June 17, 1882	Grinnell and Malcolm, Iowa	68
April 14, 1886	St. Cloud and Sauk Rapids, Minnesota	72
March 27, 1890	Kentucky, in and around Louisville	76
July 6, 1893	Pomeroy, Iowa	71
May 15, 1896	Sherman, Texas	73
May 27, 1896	St. Louis, Missouri, and St. Louis, Illinois	255
June 12, 1899	New Richmond, Wisconsin	117
May 18, 1902	Goliad, Texas	114
May 10, 1905	Oklahoma around Snyder	97
April 24, 1908	Louisiana and Mississippi	more than 91 dead
March 8, 1909	Brinkley, Arkansas	49
March 23, 1913	Nebraska and Iowa	103
May 26, 1917	Central Illinois	101
April 20, 1920	Mississippi and Alabama	88
May 2, 1920	Peggs, Oklahoma	71
April 15, 1921	Texas and Arkansas	59
June 28, 1924	Ohio, around Sandusky and Lorain	85
April 12, 1927	Rock Springs, Texas	74
May 9, 1927	Arkansas and Missouri	98
April 5, 1936	Tupelo, Mississippi	216
April 6, 1936	Gainesville, Georgia	203
March 16, 1942	Southern Mississippi	63
April 27, 1942	Pryor, Oklahoma	52
June 12, 1942	Oklahoma City, Oklahoma	35
June 23, 1944	Central West Virginia	111
April 12, 1945	Antlers, Oklahoma	69
April 9, 1947	Texas and Oklahoma	181
January 3, 1949	Warren, Arkansas	55
March 21, 1952	Judsonia, Arkansas	50
May 11, 1953	San Angelo and Waco, Texas	114
May 25, 1955	Udall, Kansas	80
May 20, 1957	Kansas and Missouri	44
May 15, 1968	Arkansas	35
February 21, 1971	Louisiana and Mississippi	46
April 3, 1974	Xenia, Ohio	34
April 10, 1979	Wichita Falls, Texas	42
May 22, 1987	Reeves County, Texas	30

Chapter Notes

Chapter 1. Night of Terror

1. *Today,* NBC television, April 29, 1991, from Burrelle's Transcripts, p. 4.

2. *Twister: Fury in the Plains,* The Learning Channel (TLC), 1997.

3. Ibid.

4. Ibid.

5. *Today,* NBC television, April 29, 1991, from Burrelle's transcripts, p. 4.

6. Ibid.

7. *CBS Evening News,* Interview by CBS news correspondent James Hattori, April 28, 1991, Burelle's transcripts, p. 4.

8. *CBS Evening News,* April 27, 1991, in Burrelle's transcripts, p. 1.

Chapter 2. Whirling Windstorms

1. Quoted in Peter Miller, "Tornado!" *National Geographic,* June 1987, p. 696.

2. Author interview with Thomas Edward, July 6, 1997.

3. Keay Davidson, *Twister: The Science of Tornadoes and the Making of an Adventure Movie* (New York: Simon & Schuster, 1996), p. 41.

4. Ibid., p. 25.

Chapter 3. Running for Cover

1. Taken from *Our History* [Information sheet], McConnell Air Force Base, U.S. Air Force, 1997.

2. *CBS Evening News,* April 27, 1991, from Burrelle's transcripts, p. 1.

3. "Kansas Town Giving Its Best to Aid Victims," *The New York Times,* April 29, 1991, p. A10.

4. *Today,* NBC television, April 29, 1991, from Burelle's transcripts, p. 5.

5. *Twister: Fury in the Plains,* The Learning Channel (TLC), 1997.

Chapter 4. "Everybody Cares"

1. CBS television, *CBS This Morning,* April 28, 1991, in Burrelle's transcripts, p. 2.

2. Ibid.

3. "Kansas Town Giving Its Best to Aid Victims," *The New York Times*, April 29, 1991, p. A10.

4. *CBS This Morning*, p. 4.

5. "Kansas Town Giving Its Best to Aid Victims," p. A10.

6. Ibid.

7. *CBS This Morning*, p. 4.

8. "Kansas Town Giving Its Best to Aid Victims," p. A10.

9. *NBC News at Sunrise*, April 30, 1991.

10. "Kansas Town Giving Its Best to Aid Victims," p. A10.

Chapter 5. Restoring Communities

1. *A Guide to Tornado Video Classics, 1* (St. Johnsbury, Vt.: The Tornado Project, 1996), p. 40.

2. "Kansas Town Giving Its Best to Aid Victims," *The New York Times*, April 29, 1991, p. A10.

3. *CBS This Morning*, April 28, 1991, from Burrelle's transcripts, p. 4.

4. *Our History* [information sheet], McConnell Air Force Base, U.S. Air Force, 1997.

5. Ibid.

6. Keay Davidson, *Twister: The Science of Tornadoes and the Making of an Adventure Movie* (New York: Simon & Schuster, 1996), p. 4.

7. *A Guide to Tornado Video Classics, 1* (St. Johnsbury, Vt.: The Tornado Project, 1996), p. 40.

8. Davidson, p. 24.

9. Ibid., p. 52.

10. Billie Walker Brown and Walter R. Brown, *Historical Catastrophes: Hurricanes and Tornadoes* (Reading, Mass.: Addison-Wesley, 1972), p. 196.

11. Quoted in Peter Miller, "Tornado!" *National Geographic*, June 1987, p. 703.

12. Ibid., p. 713.

13. Ibid.

14. *CBS Evening News*, April 27, 1991, from Burelle's transcripts, p. 1.

funnel cloud—A dark twisting cloud at the center of a tornado. It sucks up big and small objects in its path.

hailstones—Chunks of ice that fall from the sky similar to a rainstorm. They can become as large as tennis balls or even grapefruits.

multiple vortex tornadoes—Tornadoes that contain more than one circulation spinning around their middle.

single vortex tornadoes—Tornadoes that contain only one circulation spinning around their middle.

storm chasers—People who follow the paths of tornadoes. These people hope to get close enough to the tornadoes to film them.

Tornado Alley—The region of the United States with the most frequent tornado activity. It begins in Texas and moves north into Oklahoma, Kansas, and Iowa.

tornadoes—Circular windstorms that come from thunderstorms.

Books

Archer, Jules. *Tornado!* Columbus, Ohio: Silver Burdett Press, 1991.

Armbruster, Ann, and Elizabeth A. Taylor. *Tornadoes.* New York: Franklin Watts, 1989.

Cleary, Margot Keam. *Great Disasters of the Twentieth Century.* New York: Gallery Books, 1990.

Davidson, Keay. *Twister: The Science of Tornadoes and the Making of an Adventure Movie.* New York: Pocket Books, 1996.

Davis, Lee. *Natural Disasters.* New York: Facts on File, 1992.

Grazulis, Thomas P. *Significant Tornadoes: 1680–1991.* St. Johnsbury, Vt.: The Tornado Project, 1991.

Greenberg, Keith Elliot. *Stormchaser.* Woodbridge, Ct.: Blackbirch Press, 1997.

Hopping, Loraine Jean. *Tornadoes!* New York: Scholastic, 1994.

Keller, David. *Great Disasters: The Most Shocking Moments in History.* New York: Avon, 1990.

Kramer, Stephen. *Eye of the Storm: Chasing Storms With Warren Faidley.* New York: Putnam's, 1997.

Internet Sources

The Tornado Project
<http://www.tornadoproject.com>

Stormchasers
<http://taiga.geog.niu.edu/chaser/chaser.html>

National Severe Storms Laboratory
<http://www.nssl.uoknor.edu>

Videos

Nature's Fury, National Geographic Society, 1995.

Tornado Video Classics, 1, The Tornado Project, 1992.

Index